This book belongs to

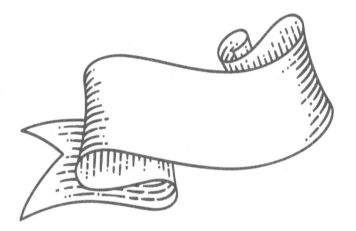

Contents

What are shortcuts?

A shortcut is basically a way of doing something on your computer that will speed up the process.

For example, if you want to copy some text and paste it somewhere else, you can highlight the text, go to edit, then choose copy, go to your next document, go to edit and then choose paste. Sure, this isn't too hard to do, but if you simply press the Ctrl button and the letter C, it'll copy it automatically (you might say automagically – or you might not). Then, press Ctrl and the letter V and it'll paste your text. That's a shortcut.

Start menu

Press the windows key on your keyboard and the start menu will open. Prime example of a short cut, you might as well take the batteries out of your mouse and put them in your tv remote. You can also press Ctrl followed by the esc button if you fancy a stretch.

Secondary Start Menu

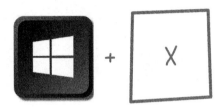

Oh, so you don't like the fancy start menu? That's okay, press the Windows key and X to get the secondary start menu up.

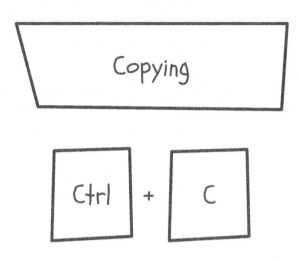

Copying

Ctrl + C

If you highlight something you want to copy, such as some text or a picture, hold down Ctrl and C, and it'll copy it to your clipboard.

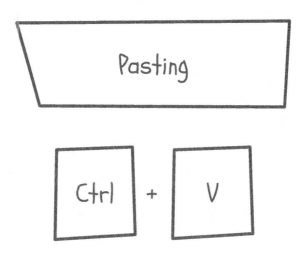

Pasting

Ctrl + V

Once you've got something copied to your clipboard, you can paste it into another document or program by using this handy shortcut. Just hold down Ctrl and V together. Voilà!

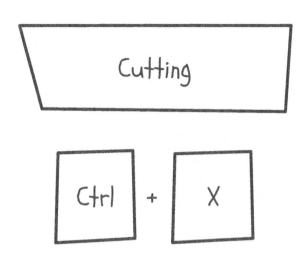

Cutting

Ctrl + X

Let's say you don't want to copy your text and paste it in another document. Let's say you want to move it completely and delete it from the original place. Well, cut it instead of copying it.

Pressing Ctrl and X together will remove the text from the place it is originally. Then, you can Ctrl V it elsewhere.

Paste clipboard

+ V

Copied more than one thing?

If you have copied (Ctrl+C) lots of different text and even images, you can press the windows key + V and the paste clipboard will come up so you can choose what to paste (Ctrl+V) from a list of your copied items!

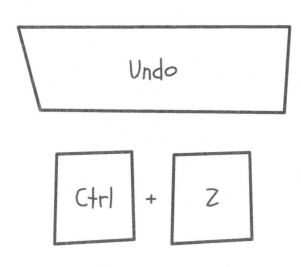

Oops! You've made a mistake.

But panic not, for there is the mother of all shortcuts here to help you out. Pressing Ctrl and Z together will undo the last action you did on your computer. Phew!!!

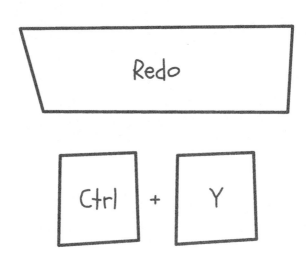

Oops! You've gone too far.

If you were just undoing all of your mistakes in life, and undid one too many, you can pop it back in. Press Ctrl + Y and it will add back in what you just took out by mistake!

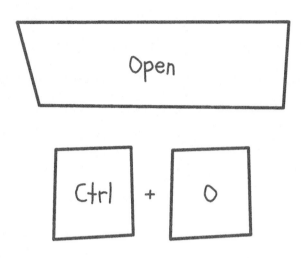

Open

Ctrl + O

Are you in Word or something but can't be bothered to go to file and open? Just press Ctrl and O, it'll do the hard work for you!

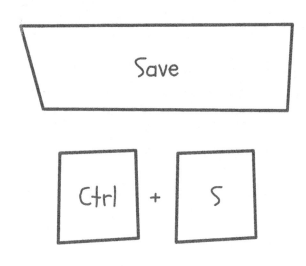

To be honest, after hearing all of the horror stories where people have lost hours and days and weeks and months worth of work, you should have autosave set up, but if you like to live life on the edge, and want to be in control of when things are saved, just press Ctrl and S to save your work.

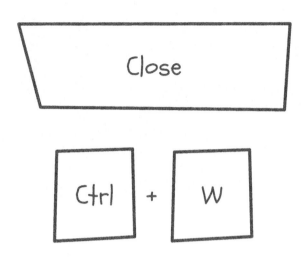

Eugh, who can be bothered to go all the way to the top of the screen, move the cursor all the way to the right hand side, and then click on the cross? Not me!

Instead, just press Ctrl and W together and it'll close whatever you have open.

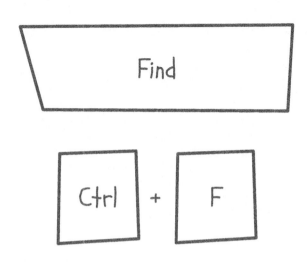

Find

Ctrl + F

If you're looking at a wall of text and only want to find one particular word, press Ctrl and F to bring up the find box. Then just type in what you're looking for, and press enter!

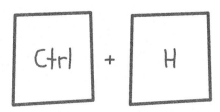

Find & replace

Ctrl + H

Have you just created a whole document and spelt someone's name wrong? Don't worry, press Ctrl + H to bring up the find and replace box to correct the error!

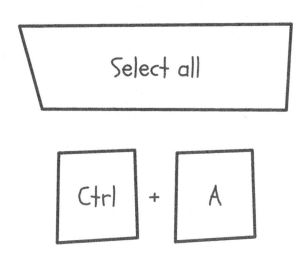

Select all

Ctrl + A

If you press Ctrl and A together, it'll select everything in that document or web browser – all the text, images, everything!

You can then Ctrl C it and Ctrl V it elsewhere if you need to.

Print screen

PrtScn

If you want to capture an image of the whole screen that you're looking at, press the print screen button (PrtScn) on your keyboard, and then Ctrl and V to paste it where you'd like!

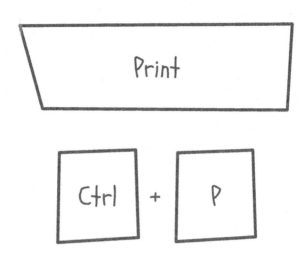

To bring up your printing options as quick as a flash, hold down Ctrl and press P together. This will bring up your choices so you can choose the printer, lay out, and print your documents!

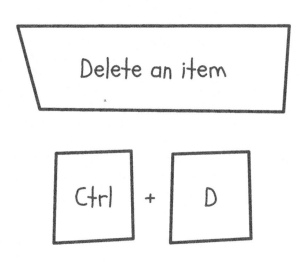

Delete an item

Ctrl + D

If you want to delete an item, highlight it and press Ctrl + D, just the delete button can work for this one if you can bothered to reach for it.

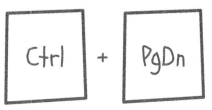

Page down

Ctrl + PgDn

If you're like me and find scrolling up and down pages tedious, simply hold Ctrl and press PgDn and you'll jump to the end of your page in a second!

You might have to turn Num Lock off for this one.

Page Up

Ctrl + PgUp

Having just seen the Page Down shortcut, you might have worked out Page Up, but for all those at the back, IF YOU WANT TO SCROLL UP FAST, PRESS CTRL + PgUp AT THE SAME TIME!

Sorry for shouting, but don't forget you might need to turn Num Lock off for this one to work.

Minimise all windows

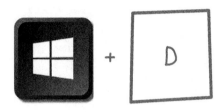

If you're a busy bee and you find that you have all of the windows open that your device has to offer but you need to get to your desktop sharpish, you don't have to minimise each and every one, thank goodness! Simply press the Windows key and press D at the same time, and you'll be looking at your desktop quicker than you can say "I've got a lot of windows open". Press the same again to bring them back up!

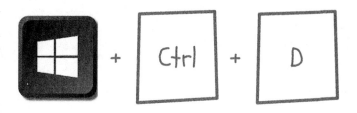

Virtual Desktop

⊞ + Ctrl + D

In fact, if you have a lot of windows open, why don't you separate your tasks and plan that secret birthday party on a completely separate desktop? Press the Windows key + Ctrl + D and keep things nice and easy.

Virtual Desktop Navigation

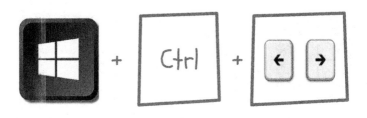

Don't worry, you can swap between the two quickly by pressing the Windows key + Ctrl and the left or right arrow to move between virtual desktops, or as I like to call them, secret birthday planning areas.

Switch between windows (quick)

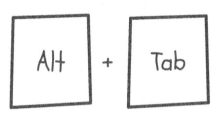

Alt + Tab

If you find you're swapping between two or more windows quite often, just press Alt and Tab to swap between them quickly. Hold alt and tap tab until you find the window you want to bring forwards, then let go! This works well if you're just swapping between two windows quickly.

Switch between windows (relax)

| Ctrl | + | Alt | + | Tab |

This is very similar to the Alt + tab option but this combo brings up all of your open windows and leaves them on display for you. Now you can move your arrows to choose which window you want to make full screen and pressing enter, or just click it.

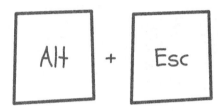

Cycle through windows

Alt + Esc

This one is also very similar to Alt + tab where you can flip between different windows you have open, but Alt and Esc cycles through the windows you have open in the order you opened them.

Move your window

Instead of clicking and dragging your window all over the screen, just hold down the windows key and one of the arrows to move it to the left or the right. Windows key and the down arrow restores down the screen, and the up arrow puts it back full size!

Open task view

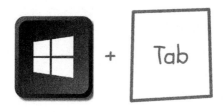

+ Tab

If you want to have a look at your task view, press the windows key and tab. It'll show you what you have open and what you've had open. You can also close down your virtual desktops/secret party planning areas here.

Languages installed

 + Spacebar

If you're incredibly smart and can speak/type in different languages and have them set up on your computer, press the Windows key and the spacebar to select which language you fancy today.

Emojis

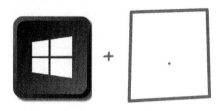

That's Windows key and the full stop to you and I. Press those together to open up the emoji menu so you can let people know how you really feel.

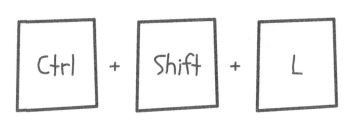

New bullet point

Ctrl + Shift + L

Typing away in Word and suddenly need to bullet point some trade secrets? Press Ctrl + Shift + L to start them off!

Insert hyperlink

Ctrl + K

Want to insert a hyperlink somewhere? Press Ctrl and K and insert one then!

Highlighting words

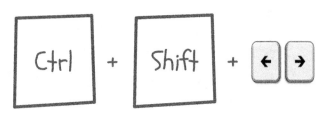

Ctrl + Shift + ← →

If you want to highlight a few words but can't be bothered to find your mouse and click and drag (yawn), press Ctrl + Shift and the left or right arrow to highlight the next word in line. Then you can Ctrl + C and Ctrl V where you please.

Highlighting lines

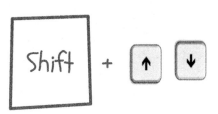

Have a wall of text that you need to get highlighted quickly but only a select few lines? Press shift and the up or down arrow, depending on your preferred direction, to highlight lines.

Move your cursor

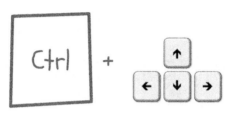

Ctrl +

You can move your cursor around the local area without highlighting the text in between travels. Just press Ctrl and the up or down arrow to jump up and down lines and paragraphs. You can press Ctrl and left or right to jump between words, too.

File explorer

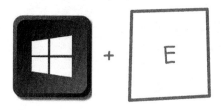 + E

Press the Windows key and E to open file explorer...it's that easy.

Cortana

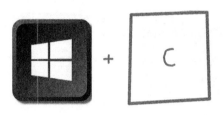

+ C

Press the Windows key and C to open up Cortana in listening mode and ask her something pressing, like, 'How's the weather in Japan?'

Windows Search

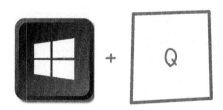 + Q

This could be the Windows key and C but it depends if you have Cortana. Press the Windows key and Q and start typing in your Windows search bar.

Apps on the taskbar

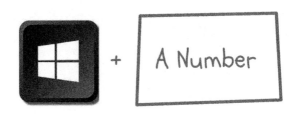

+ A Number

Have a look at your task bar at the bottom of your screen. Can you see a selection of apps? Well if you press the Windows key and the number the app is in that line, it'll open. Is file explorer 3rd in line? Press the Windows key and 3. What's just opened? You're welcome.

Xbox game bar

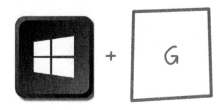 + G

Do you have an evening of gaming planned? Well press the Windows key and G to bring up the Xbox game bar and get going!

Open run dialog box

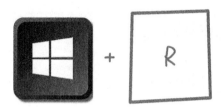

Want to show off and open a program like a professional? Press the Windows key followed by R to open the run dialog box. You can always search 'Run' in the start menu though and look like a newbie if you want to.

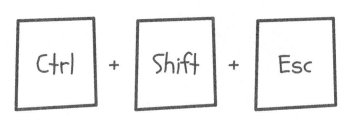

Task manager

Ctrl + Shift + Esc

Now we're on a roll. Press Ctrl, then shift then esc to open task manager. Or go for the classic Ctrl + Alt + Del THEN choose task manager. Why not save some time? Do it this new, cool way.

Settings

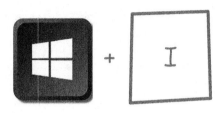

+ I

No need to go to the start menu and find Settings anymore, or type Settings into the search bar. Just press the windows key and I and you'll be ready to make some changes!

Settings menu – Ease of access

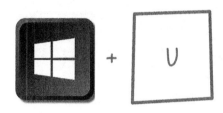

Press the Windows key and U (the letter you) to open up the settings menu, but specifically, the ease of access menu. Is it ironic that you've easily accessed the ease of access menu with a nifty new shortcut?

Dictation toolbar

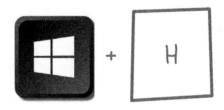

⊞ + H

If you're wearing your keyboard out with all these great new shortcuts you've learnt, but have a mountain of notes to type up, just dictate them! Press the Windows key and H and start talking.

Feedback Hub

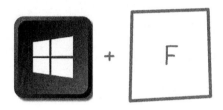 + F

Do you have a few choice words for Bill? Or a brilliant idea that he has to hear about? Press the Windows key and the letter F and pass on your fresh new ideas.

Action Centre

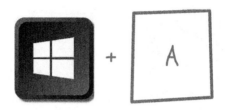

If you want a quick peek at the Action Centre, press the windows key followed by A, and you'll be peeking quickly at the Action Centre.

Projection

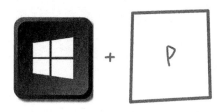

If you have far too much information on your screen and it simply will not fit comfortably, get a second monitor and press the Windows key and P to make life easier.

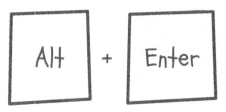

View properties

Alt + Enter

If you're looking at a selection of items in file explorer and you want to know the properties of one in particular, just highlight it and press Alt + Enter. No need to right click and select 'properties' anymore.

Lock your PC

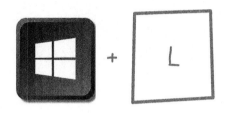

Nipping for a liquid lunch? Don't forget to lock your computer so no one reads your personal documents. Hold down the Windows key and press L. This is quicker than finding lock PC through the start menu!

Forwards/backwards

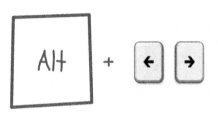

Browsing the internet and want to time travel to previous pages? Just press Alt and the left arrow, and if you want to come back this way, press Alt and the right arrow. That will take you backwards and forwards through your visited web pages.

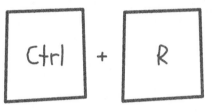

Refresh/reload a page

Ctrl + R

If you're browsing the internet and you need to refresh the page you're looking at, press Ctrl and R and it'll refresh it for you!

Search in a browser

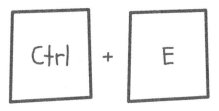

If you're looking at a webpage and want to search for something brand new, press Ctrl + E and start typing.

Word processing shortcuts

The following shortcuts work in most word processing programs such as Microsoft Word.

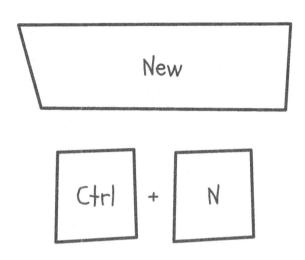

New

Ctrl + N

I think by now, none of us can be bothered to go all the way to file and find New, just press Ctrl and N to bring up a new document or page.

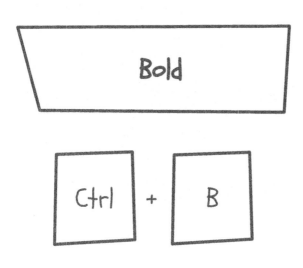

Bold

Ctrl + B

In **most** word processing programs, like **Word**, you can highlight text, press **Ctrl and B** and it will change that text to **bold**. You can press it again to take the bold off! You can press Ctrl + B **before you start tying as well to switch bold on** and off.

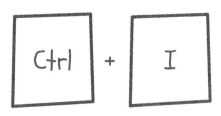

This is for most word processing programs again. You can press Ctrl and I to turn Italics on or off. It's the same as bold where you can highlight and press Ctrl and I, or press it before you start typing to switch it on or off.

Underline

Ctrl + U

You know the drill by now. <u>Most</u> word processing programs let you press Ctrl and U when you have text <u>highlighted</u> to switch <u>underline on</u> or off, or press it before you <u>start typing to switch it on</u> or off.

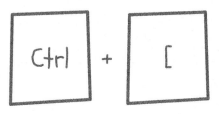

Decrease a font size

Ctrl + [

That's Ctrl and left bracket, but not the nice curved bracket, the the one that looks like a staple. Pressing this combo decreases your font size by one, press again to go down, and so on!

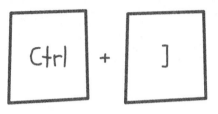

Increase a font size

Ctrl +]

This one is the backwards looking staple bracket. Press Ctrl and the right bracket to increase the font size by one. Press over and over to keep increasing!

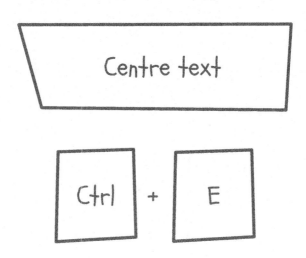

Centre text

Ctrl + E

To pop your text in the middle of the page for more

attention

press Ctrl and E.

Align text left

Ctrl + L

If you're writing a glowing review of this book and want to show off your new shortcut skills, press Ctrl and L to align the text to the left of the page.

Align text right

Ctrl + R

If you're adding your address to a formal letter, press Ctrl and R to align text right...if people still do that.

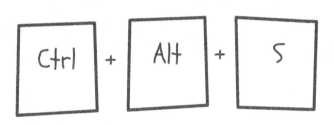

Split document window

Ctrl + Alt + S

If you want to split your Word doc window into two, press Ctrl + Alt + S, and it'll place the horizontal split bar on the screen for you. Press it again to remove the split.

Shortcuts for spreadsheets

The following shortcuts are for spreadsheets.

Remove cell contents

Delete

If you have a cell or cells with content in that you want to remove, highlight the cell or cells and press delete on your keyboard. Just make sure the cell is only highlighted and you're not in edit mode (edit mode = double clicked into the cell).

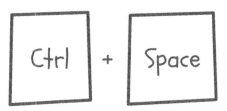

Highlight full column

Ctrl + Space

If you want to highlight a whole column but don't have the energy to click the letter at the top, press Ctrl and the spacebar.

Highlight full row

Shift + Space

If you want to highlight a whole row, press shift and the spacebar and it will highlight the whole row of the cell you're sitting in.

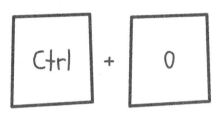

Hide selection of columns

Ctrl + 0

That's Ctrl and a zero, not the letter O. If you press that, you'll open up a new sheet, but you knew that already, right? To hide a section of columns, highlight the ones you want to hide and press Ctrl and 0 (zero, the number).

Hide selection of rows

Ctrl + 9

Make sure your rows are highlighted and press Ctrl and the number 9. This will hide the rows you want to keep secret!

Thanks for reading

I hope you found this book useful and learnt some new keyboard shortcuts ready to use and show off to all your mates!

I don't know if you noticed the shortcut directing you towards your language keyboard, but don't forget to learn a new language with 3 Minute Languages.

Printed in Great Britain
by Amazon

34131529R00046